Disney

HANNAH MONTANA

This Hannah Montana
Annual belongs to

....

Age:

What's

Inside

Meet Miley

Miley Stewart is a normal teenage girl. Except, unlike most other teenage girls, she has a secret double life as a world-famous pop star – Hannah Montana!

FACTFILE

Full name: Miley Stewart

Lives with: Dad, Robby, and brother, Jackson

Best Friends: Lilly Truscott and Oliver Oken

Style: Lots of layers, fashionable and super-girly

Likes: Going to the beach, hanging out with her friends and being a secret pop star at night!

Dislikes: Spiders and the dentist

Here's Hannah

Only a few people know that Hannah Montana is really Miley Stewart by day – and she intends to keep it that way.

FACTFILE

Full name: Hannah Montana

Best Friends: Lola Luftnagle and Mike Standley III

Style: Glamorous, funky, rock star-chic

Likes: Music and fashion

Dislikes: Carrots! (Remember when she tells Mack and Mindy during an interview and all her fans stop eating carrots?!)

Dear Hannah
Your music totally rocks!
I love your clothes too, especially your glittery skirts and fingerless glove.
Jessie x

Dear Hannah
Your dancing is awesome and I listen to your songs every day. You're the best – keep rockin' out forever!
From Amy xx

Your World

Have you ever dreamed of leading a double life? Write about yourself here, then draw a picture of your alter ego!

ABOUT YOU

Name ....

Friends ....

Family ....

Style ....

Likes ....

Dislikes ....

....

YOUR ALTER EGO

Draw yourself as your alter ego here.

Name ....

Style Spot

Hannah and her friends all have their own unique style. Can you tell who's who from the close-ups below?

LOLA

OLIVER

ROBBY

HANNAH

JACKSON

Acting Up

Act out these three scenes from, 'Judge Me Tender', using the script below. Take it in turns to play different roles with your friends.

Scene 1

JUDGE ME TENDER

Hannah is a guest judge on the reality show, 'America's Top Talent'. She can't believe it when Oliver auditions – Oliver and Lilly had kept it a secret! But will he blow her away with his singing?

Andy: So my man, in honour of our guest judge here, which Hannah song you gonna drop on us tonight?

Oliver: The brilliant, 'Let's Do This'. Of course, all of her songs are brilliant, because she's such a great artist. (Hannah shifts uncomfortably in her seat.) And, so I hear, kind and caring and forgiving . . .

Hannah: And hates surprises – just in case you were wondering! (Arms folded.)

Byron: Do you know what I was wondering? If you're going to sing before Andy's head starts sprouting stubble!

The music starts over and Oliver bursts into song. Hannah can't help but sing along to herself 'cos Oliver's performance is brilliant. Andy and Byron look really impressed. Lola, who's backstage, and the audience absolutely love it!

Andy: You know what I can't resist? Telling you, you have talent. Good job.

Hannah: Way to go Oliver . . . (Hannah stands up in excitement, then remembers she's not supposed to know Oliver) Oken. Oliver Oken! Yep, never heard that name before. Very interesting! I'd say it's my first Oken. Kinda like Token Oken! (Laughs.) You know, for just hearing his name for the first time today, I think that's pretty darn clever. (Fans herself with a programme.) OK, Byron?

Byron: Well, Mr Oken, I have to say I find myself completely appalled . . . (Hannah screws up her face, while Lola looks worried) by how much I like that. Well done! (Oliver looks shocked and very pleased.)

Hannah: Well done! You were so much better than you were at that (Hannah points exitedly, then pulls back) at the beginning, where I thought you were just a *leetle* pitchy. But, good job, Otto. (Andy and Byron look at Hannah.) See, I don't even know his name, cause I've never met him before! Is it a commercial yet?

The next day at school, Lilly wants to make sure that Miley is OK with Oliver appearing on 'America's Top Talent'. Miley tells her that as long as she knows that their friendship can't influence her vote, then it's all cool.

Lilly: He'd never want you to play favourites, because that's the kind of friend he is. A good friend, a best friend, a friend who would never let you down.

Miley: Oh cool, for a minute there I thought you were going to pressure me or something!

Lilly: I'm sorry, I just really want him to win.

Miley: And he will, if he's the best. You know, I'm just so surprised that you're on board with this, I mean, considering how it could affect your relationship.

Lilly: Our relationship, what do you mean? (Right on cue, a hoard of screaming girl fans chase Oliver and corner him. They make him sing, before dragging him away, leaving Miley and Lilly squashed up against a locker.) OK, I know what you're thinking, OK? But my Ollie-pop and I have a very strong, trusting relationship and I'm totally not worried, I mean just because girls are going to be all over him, it doesn't mean he's going to be affected by it.

Later on at Rico's Surf Shack, Lilly is putting suntan lotion on Miley. Oliver comes in, wearing sunglasses. He's being chased by more girls and is absolutely loving it!

Miley: Are you sure you're OK with this?

Lilly: Yeah, yeah, I'm fine! I mean, he's just having fun with all the new attention. I mean, it's not like he's treating *me* any different.

Oliver: Hey babe, the fans want to take pictures of me by the ocean, so I'll call you, babe. To the beach! (Cue screams from his fans as they head for the ocean.)

Lilly: He called me babe! Twice! (She starts rubbing suntan lotion really hard into Miley's shoulders.)

Miley: Ow, ow, OW!

Lilly: I'm sorry. Sorry! I was just trying to rub it in.

Miley: To what? My bones?

Lilly: Miley, what am I going to do? That show's turning my Ollie popstar into an Ollie poostar.

Miley: OK, I know we agreed that we'd never say, 'I told you so,' so I'm going to text you, OK? (Starts texting Lilly.)

Lilly: Miley? (Lilly's phone beeps.)

Miley: What? I'm just so fast! Look, if I could just, you know, boot him off, I would.

Lilly: Why, can't you? (Smiling as if to say, 'Do it, Miley!')

Miley: As soon as he doesn't do a good job, I'm going to drop-kick his 'Babe Oken' butt right out of the studio!

Lilly: But wait, what if he keeps being good?

Miley: Oh come on, Lilly, let's not dwell on the positive!

Lilly: So you'd vote for him again, even after the way he's treating me?

Miley: Well, I'd have to. I mean, I couldn't say he was bad if he wasn't. I mean, we all agreed that I'd vote conscientiously.

Lilly: Do you have that in writing?

Miley: Lilly!

Lilly: Well, what's more important? Your conscience, or my happiness?

Miley: Well, that's not really fair, because technically it's not my conscience, it's Hannah Montana's. And you know, that has to do with, you know, all corporate things – you know, contracts, legal stuff, yadda yadda yadda. Very complicated.

Lilly: Well, I'll tell you something that's not complicated. A friend would vote Oliver off and if you can't do that for me . . . well, then I guess we're not as close as I thought. (Walks off with mobile phone.)

Miley: Oh come on, Lilly, you can't be that mad! (Phone beeps with a text from Lilly.) Oooh, she really is that mad!

Do you remember what happens next? Miley tries to talk to Oliver about neglecting Lilly, but he's so caught up in being a popstar, he doesn't listen. She tries to give him a bad review at the next show, but he's so good that Lola gives her permission to put him through to the semi finals. After the show, she talks to Oliver again and he finally realises how badly he's been acting. He and Lilly make up after he gives her a huge apology!

Miley's Music

Miley and her alter ego, Hannah, are mad about music.
Can you find ten musical words in the grid below?

Words go forwards, up, down and diagonally!

```
W J S I N G E R W C P E
G P T W W F Y H I R N R
S U I G T U N E N O I G
Y O I A Z Q W Y H W K X
S E N T N X D P Y D Q M
Y T V G A O O L K D T E
Z J A O W R U P S R B N
N T R G C R P G E T W C
Z U E I E E I C F Q H O
I M M N D V N T P P N R
N K H D R O R T E N E E
S R Y N C F J L O R X O
```

GUITAR

STAGE

MICROPHONE

PIANO

SINGER

CROWD

SONGWRITER

CONCERT

ENCORE

TUNE

Answers on page 67.

16

five Things

There are five differences in the second picture
of Lola, Hannah and Jackson. Can you find them all?

**Tick a star
when you spot
each difference!**

1

2

3

4

5

Answers on page 67.

Best Friends Forever

Miley, Lilly and Oliver are the best of buddies but, like all friends, they have the odd fall out too! Read their tips on how to be the best friend ever . . .

Friends First

It's not always easy having an international pop star as a best friend, but Miley always tries to put her friends first. In 'Can't Get Home to You, Girl', she goes to crazy lengths to get back from an out-of-state concert in time for Lilly's birthday. A sign of true friendship!

The Extra Mile

In, 'What I Don't Like About You', Miley finds out that Lilly and Oliver are dating, but haven't told her! When she tells them that she knows, they argue, break up and ask her to take sides! So Miley helps them to forgive each other.

No Lies

Miley told Lilly a white lie when she paid for someone to buy Lilly's hat from her, so that she could afford the school trip in, 'Would I Lie To You, Lilly?'. Lilly found out and was really upset. Miley made it up to her when she said she was more like her sister than her best friend.

Making Mistakes

In 'You Gotta Lose This Job', Oliver gets upset about Hannah always getting what she wants. She tries to fail an audition on purpose, but it backfires and Oliver realises how much his friendship means to her when she gives up her part in the film. Aw!

Hannah's Top Friendship Tips

✴ Listen to your friends when they feel sad. A problem shared is a problem halved!

✴ Show how much pals mean to you by making them friendship bracelets or writing them poems.

✴ Have a giggle together – it's an instant mood-lifter!

✴ Be honest with your bezzies and tell them if they've upset you, then try and work it out together.

Glamour Montana

Check out these top tips for looking super-stylish, the Hannah Montana way!

Dare to be different! Glue gems onto the frames of your sunglasses for rockstar-glam!

Wear what you like and feel comfortable in. Hannah loves her black jacket!

Find one signature accessory. Hannah's pink fingerless glove is super-funky!

Remember, fab accessories can totally make a look pop!

Sleepover Fun

Try these fun games for an awesome Hannah Montana-themed sleepover!

You and your friends can dress up as Hannah, Lola, Miley or Lilly. Bring CDs and DVDs and play these awesome girly games!

Guess Who?

Choose which Hannah character you're going to pretend to be. Your friends then take it in turn to ask questions to work out who you are. You can only answer 'yes' or 'no'. The person who guesses the most characters correctly, wins!

Totally Cool Quiz

Test your Hannah knowledge with our quiz on page 64! Choose one person to ask the questions and give a forfeit to anyone who gets a question wrong.

22

Hannah-oke!
Take it in turns to sing your favourite Hannah songs. Choose one of your friends to be a judge – just like Hannah on 'America's Top Talent'.

Choose a picture to describe to your friends.

cake

house

beetle

Pass the Microphone

Use a hairbrush if you haven't got a microphone. Say a Hannah Montana related word, then pass the microphone to the person on your right. They have to say a word which relates to that word, before passing the microphone on to the next person, who does the same. If you make a mistake, you're out. Carry on until there's only one girl left with the microphone – she's the winner!

sheep

Draw It

Take it in turns to choose a picture from the column on the right and describe it to the others without using the actual word. Your friends try to draw what you are describing. The winner is the one whose picture is closest to the one being described. You'll get a few funny pics to make you chuckle!

ice cream

23

It's Lilly

Fun-loving, excitable Lilly is Miley and Oliver's best friend. She also has a secret double life ...

FACTFILE

Full name: Lillian Truscott (Lilly)

Lives with: Mom, Heather

Style: Laid-back, sassy, surfer girl

Likes: Skateboarding, surfing and cheerleading

Dislikes: Being ill on her birthday!

Introducing Lola

Lola Luftnagle is Lilly's alias! She travels to concerts with Hannah and acts as her assistant.

FACTFILE

Full name: Lola Luftnagle

Best Friend: Hannah Montana

Style: Clashing colours, bright wigs and lots of accessories

Likes: Helping Hannah keep her secret identity!

Dislikes: Hannah's socialite friend, Traci Van Horn

Picture Puzzles

Are you super-sharp? Test your skills on these picture puzzles!

Face Up!

Who do each of these features belong to?

1 ___ ___ ___ ___ ___ ___

2 ___ ___ ___ ___ ___ ___

3 ___ ___ ___ ___ ___ ___

4 ___ ___ ___ ___ ___ ___

5 ___ ___ ___ ___ ___ ___ ___

Shadow Show

Which shadow matches Hannah perfectly?

A ☐

B ☐

C ☐

Answers on page 67.

Help Lola

Lola's running late for Hannah's concert!
See if you can help her through the maze
to get her there on time.

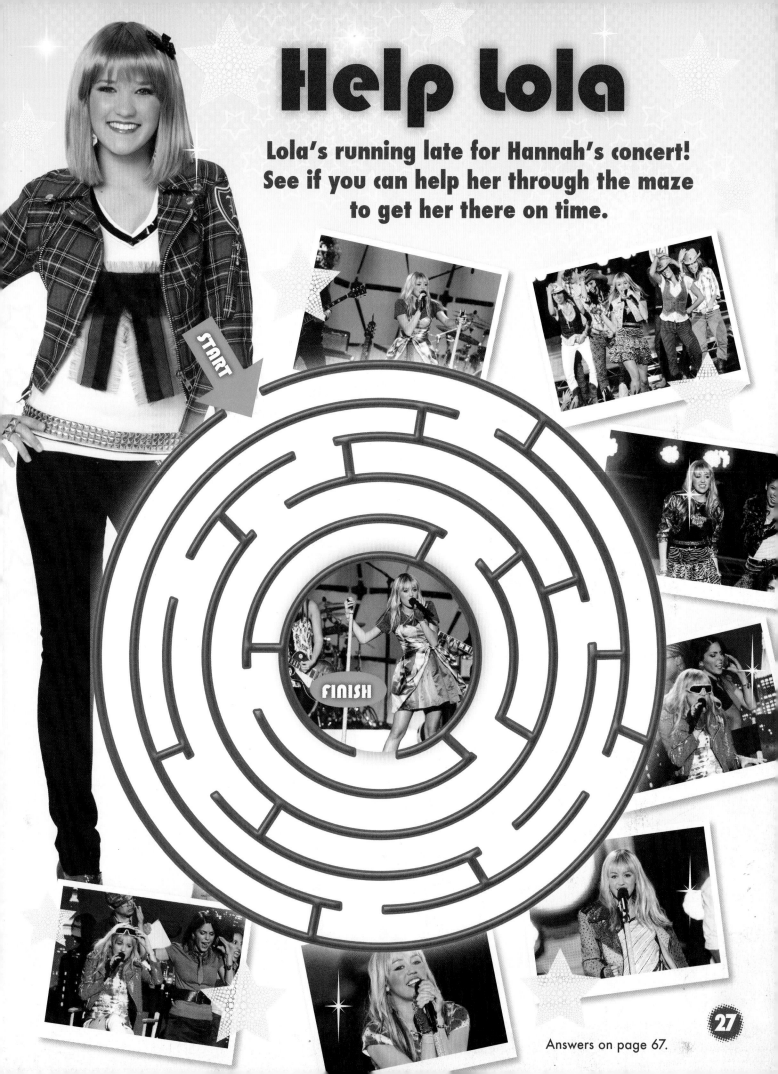

START

FINISH

Hair Bow Babe

Take on Lola's totally cute look and make it your own with a funky polka dot hair bow!

1

Cut out a rectangle from your dotted fabric. The bigger the rectangle, the bigger your bow will be. 15cm x 8cm is a cute size. Fold in the two long edges of the fabric.

2

Then fold in the short edges so they overlap. Hold in place with one finger if you need to.

3

Scrunch the centre of the rectangle in to create a bow shape, then sew a couple of stitches through the layers to fix it in place.

Make bows for your friends, too!

4

Cut out a smaller, thinner rectangle of fabric and fold in the long edges to make a narrow strip. Stitch it into a loop small enough to fit snuggly over the centre of the bow.

5

Slip the loop over one end of your bow and into the centre.

WAYS TO WEAR!

Use fabric glue to stick your bow to the side of a hairband or slip a plain grip or hair clip through the loop on the back to make a cool hair slide! Totally glam!

face facts

Your face shape and features can say a lot about your character. Find out what Hannah's face says about her!

Eyes
My eyes are deep-set, which means I'm creative and romantic!

Nose
If you're very expressive, the chances are you've got a button nose like mine!

Lips
Full lips show that I'm caring and sensitive. It's all about the pout!

Face
My face is oval, which is a sign that I'm an honest and totally open person.

Your features

EYES – If your eyes are unevenly set, you probably love to analyse things, while close-set eyes are a sign of a trustworthy person. Big eyes show imagination and small eyes are a sign of being organised.

NOSE – A small, short nose signifies kindness and long noses tend to belong to very active people.

LIPS – If you are a calm kinda gal, the chances are that you have thin lips. A fuller top lip shows a love of freedom and a fuller bottom lip signifies generosity.

FACE – Round-faced peeps like to look on the bright side, while a long face shows that you are super-observant.

Body language

Remember when Miley met Connor, a cute guy who was much shorter than her? Check out what Miley, Connor, Lilly and Oliver's body language is saying in this scene...

Lilly has narrowed her eyes and looks irritated because she spotted Connor before Miley, which also explains her hands on hips. (This was pre-Oliver!) Oliver has cocked his head to one side because he's listening to the conversation. He's not smiling either as he seems to be trying to figure out what's going on!

Miley is looking directly at Connor here and making him the object of attention because she thinks he's kinda cute! Connor is totally focused on Miley, too. His eye is holding her gaze, because he thinks she's interesting.

Miley's top tips

Three things to remember about body language!

1 **If you fold your arms** across your chest, it could be a sign that you're annoyed about something.

2 **How do you tell if someone who's smiling is really happy?** They are smiling with their eyes. (Their eyes will be totally sparkling!)

3 **If someone mirrors your actions,** it usually means that they think you're really awesome!

The Missing Link

Use the list of words below to help you complete each quote.
There is one wrong word, so watch you don't get caught out!

1

" Oliver, I'm the _ _ _ _ _ _ _!
I spread myself way to thin. "

2

" Wig? Got it!
Single _ _ _ _ _ glove?
Got it! "

3

" Smokin' Oken is
about to be
_ _ _ _ _ _ _ _. "

FRIEND	☐	PINK	☐
SWEET	☐	SLEEP	☐
ONE	☐	COLD	☐
BUTTER	☐	BROKEN	☐
HOT	☐	SUBTLE	☐

4 **❝** Like kissing a catfish. A _ _ _ _ _ , dead catfish with shiny lips. **❞**

5 **❝** She's my best _ _ _ _ _ _ _ _ and she wouldn't let me help her. **❞**

6 **❝** Even in my _ _ _ _ _ _ _ I'm smarter than you! **❞**

7 **❝** I gotta date with a _ _ _ _ _ _ niblet! **❞**

8 **❝** I got the point, Captain _ _ _ _ _ _ _ _ _. **❞**

9 **❝** I kinda think that he could be the _ _ _ _. **❞**

Answers on page 67.

Showbiz Quiz

What you would do if you were famous?
Take Hannah's celeb quiz and find out!

Start

You prefer to ask questions, rather than be asked . . .

for sure! →

Friends describe you as . . .

cheeky →

Would you have a stage name if you were famous?

↓ *no way!*

↓ *dramatic*

yes!

↓ *no!*

Would you rather star in a TV talent show or watch one?

watch! →

You totally love . . .

gossip →

You get told off at school for . . .

↓ *star!*

↓ *attention*

chatting

↓ *texting*

You drive your friends crazy by . . .

having dramas →

Do you prefer telling a story or listening to one?

listening →

Do people rely on you in sticky situations?

↓ *singing*

↓ *telling*

no!

↓ *yes!*

SASSY SINGER!

Singing is your passion and you were born to perform!

AWESOME ACTRESS

You'd make a brilliant actress, just like Miley acting out her alter ego!

PERSONAL ASSISTANT

You're super-organised and sassy, too! The perfect P.A!

34

Super Scramble!

See if you can unscramble each row of letters to reveal some funky Hannah Montana song titles. Write your answers below each row.

1

E H U L C O D E B H E T O E N

H _ / O _ _ / _ _ / H _ / _ _ _

2

I N A N A W O K N W Y U O

_ _ / _ A _ _ _ / _ / _ _ _ W / _ _ _

3

Y E V R E R T P A F O E M

E _ _ _ _ _ / _ _ T / _ _ / _ _

4

F I E W R E W E A V M E I O

_ _ _ _ / _ _ _ E / _ _ / M _ _

Answers on page 67.

35

10 Things We love about Hannah

Check out ten reasons why Hannah Montana totally rocks!

1 She's really stylish

Hannah isn't afraid to experiment with her style!

2 She loves her fans

Remember when she sang to them in a traffic jam, even though she was really tired after a show?

3 She's a great friend

Even though she's a busy pop star, Hannah never lets her friends down.

4 She's totally talented!
Her singing and dancing are super-sassy!

5 She's down-to-earth
Hannah's remained the same grounded person she always was, even though she's now an international supersstar.

6 She has a sense of humour
She's really funny and comes out with some hilarious one-liners!

7 She loves her Dad
Hannah and her dad, Robby, sometimes bicker but they're still super-close!

8 She's a brilliant actress
Remember her movie, Indiana Joanie?! Amazing!

9 She has a great life
She really has 'The Best of Both Worlds' – normal teenage life by day and crazy superstar by night!

10 She has a cute boot collection
She has the sort of shoe and boot collection most peeps could only dream about!

What's your favourite thing about Hannah? Write about it here!

37

What Kind of Friend Are You?

Are you great at giving advice, fab at being fun, or everyone's fave friend? Find out your friendship style here!

1 Your best friend has bought a new top that she loves but you don't think it suits her. Do you . . .

A Say how nice it is anyway. You'd rather not hurt her feelings. ☐

B Be honest, but point out how much all of her other tops suit her. ☐

C Try and distract her, and then change the subject. ☐

2 A pal of yours feels down in the dumps. How do you cheer her up?

A Tell her how amazing she is until she feels better. ☐

B Just be there for her with plenty of hugs and advice. ☐

C Make her giggle – laughter really is the best medicine. ☐

3 In a big group of friends, you are most likely to be . . .

A Making sure you get to speak to everyone there. ☐

B Having a long chat with one or two people. ☐

C The centre of attention with your crazy antics! ☐

4

You've fallen out with a buddy. How do you make it up to her?

A Write her a poem to say sorry. ☐

B Have a heart-to-heart and talk about why you fell out. ☐

C Make her a banner saying 'sorry' and leave it outside her house! ☐

5

Something really exciting has happened to your bezzie. What's your reaction?

A A hug. ☐

B A special congratulations speech. ☐

C A huge scream and jumping around. ☐

If you answered mostly A

Just like Oliver, you're everyone's friend. You don't like to be drawn into arguments and get on well with most people.

If you answered mostly B

Like Miley, you're a dependable and honest friend. You're always there for your buddies and give great advice.

If you answered mostly C

You're loud, outgoing and fun, just like Lilly. Deep down, you're very thoughtful and you really care about your friends.

Say What?

Can you match these quotes to the characters who said them? Write the answer in each bubble.

1

"Hotshot Hollywood honcho, say what?"

....

Clue: This character is always on the go, but always there for their friends.

2

"I have manly nose hairs. I get it from your Aunt Pearl!"

....

Clue: This character is always embarrassing the peeps closest to him!

4

"Eeep, I love being a peep!"

Clue: This person is the best friend and sidekick of our favourite songstress.

5

"You've just messed with the wrong sand crab, Missy."

Clue: This character is always falling out with the person they said this to.

3

"With this new 'do – I got the best hair in Malibu."

Clue: This character turned out to be a really great singer.

Answers on page 67.

Odd One Out

Check out these six images of Lilly and Oliver. Can you work out which picture is the odd one out and why?

Answer on page 68.

Wordwhirl

Fill in the missing words from the episode titles using the words below. The last letter of each missing word is the first letter of the next one!

Once . Twice . Three . . . . . . Video Killed the Radio Star . . . . . . the Feelings of the Radio Star . . . . . . Miley . . . . . . Don't Go Breaking My . . . . . . For (give) a little . . . . . . Don't . . . . . . Afraidy . . . . . Ready . . . . . Don't Drive

Set ★ Bit ★ Tooth ★ Times ★ Hurt

43

Answers on page 68.

Dream On

Dreams can be a bit strange, so what does it all mean? Remember when Miley dreamt that Lilly and Jackson liked each other ...

Miley's dream

Miley dreamt that Lilly and Jackson nearly kissed, then she woke up and told them both about it separately. They both admitted that they liked each other, so Miley lied to them both and pretended the other wasn't interested. But she felt so guilty about lying to her brother and best friend, that she ended up telling them the truth. Then she woke up and realised the whole thing was a dream!

So what does it mean?

Miley dreamt this because she knows she should always be honest with her friends and family, even if she thinks she won't like the outcome. It also sounds like she was practising how she would react if this was to really happen! (See the section below about why we dream.)

Everybody dreams!

You have several dreams during sleep, you just don't always remember them – freaky!

Dream time

The average person dreams for one to two hours every night.

Write it down!

Only five minutes after the end of a dream, half of it is usually forgotten!

Why do we dream?

No one really knows for sure, but there are lots of theories. Here are a few to keep you wondering …

- We dream to work out which memories to keep from the day and which memories to lose.

- Dreams don't have a purpose, it's just your brain trying to reorganise information.

- We can learn how to deal with situations by understanding how we react to them in a dream.

- They're a way of preparing us for the stuff we may experience when we wake up.

All About Jackson

Fun-loving Jackson Rod Stewart loves playing pranks and teasing little sister Miley. He's secretly very proud of her success though!

THREE THINGS WE LOVE ABOUT HIM

⭐ He does funny impressions of people, including his sister and dad!

⭐ He hasn't given up on dating, despite all of the bad dates he's had!

⭐ Underneath his jokey exterior, he's got a heart of gold.

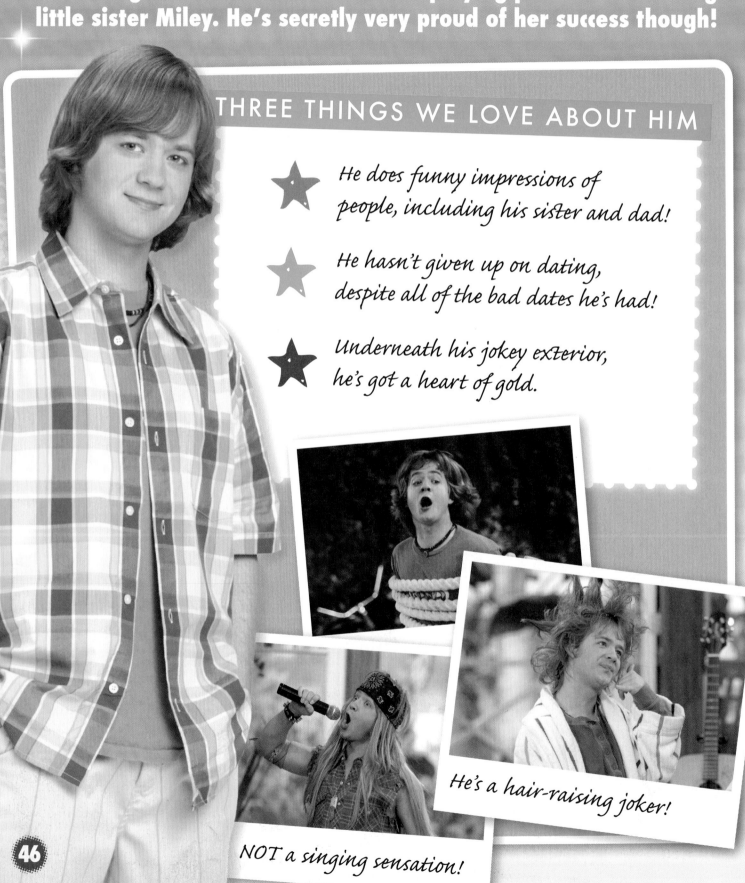

He's a hair-raising joker!

NOT a singing sensation!

It's Robby Ray

Robby is Miley and Jackson's lovable dad. Like Miley, he's a very talented singer, in fact, he used to be a country music star!

DID YOU KNOW THAT ...

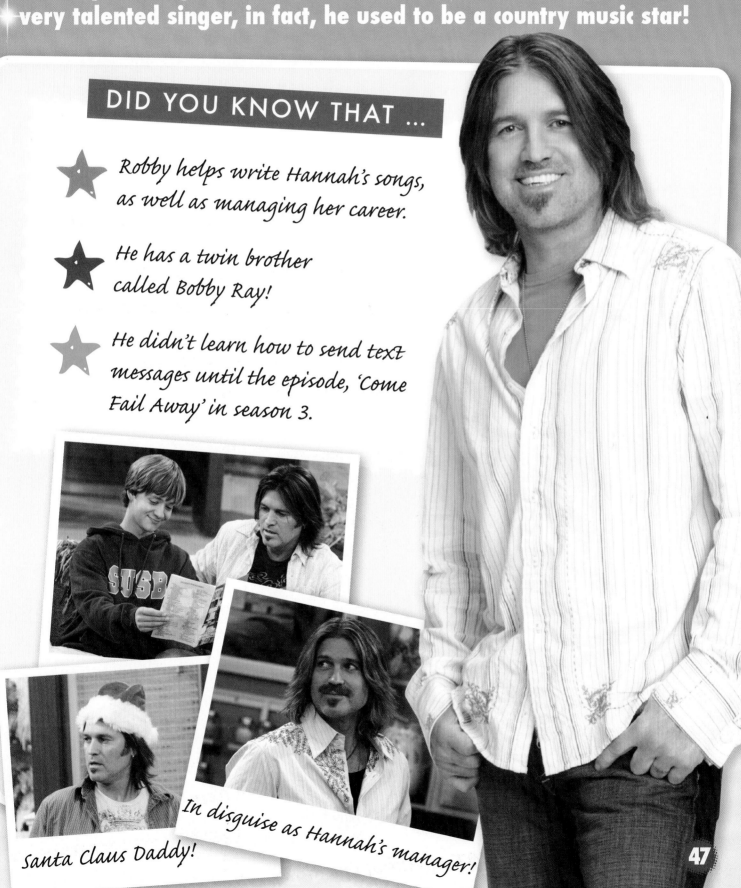

★ Robby helps write Hannah's songs, as well as managing her career.

★ He has a twin brother called Bobby Ray!

★ He didn't learn how to send text messages until the episode, 'Come Fail Away' in season 3.

Santa Claus Daddy!

In disguise as Hannah's manager!

47

Jackson & Robby's Top Cringes

Robby and Jackson get themselves into all kinds of embarrassing situations. These are some of their cringiest moments so far ...

Stop embarrassing me, Dad!

Robby takes the embarrassing father routine to a whole new level when, in season three, he tries to stop Alison finishing with Jackson. He asks Alison if they've kissed yet – eeep!

Dad's the word!

The model brother!

A model, moi?

When Jackson and Oliver are asked to model for a brochure, their egos get super-huge. But when they discover that they were only chosen because they're average-looking, they refuse to model again – until they're offered a whole lot of money. Cha-ching!

Sneezy does it

Not only is Jackson doing a ridiculous comedy laugh when he opens the door to his date Alison in 'Jake ... Another Little Piece of My Heart' but she goes to kiss him, and Jackson sneezes on her! Eww!

Sssh! It's a secret

Hannah accidentally reveals two secrets about Jackson during a radio interview – he's got fungal-infected feet and he picks his belly button – bleugh! Super-cringe!

Texting trauma

Remember when Robby learnt to text on his phone in 'Come Fail Away'? He got addicted to texting and drove Jackson crazy by constantly messaging him when he was in the middle of trying to impress a girl!

Don't sweat it – just text it!

Driving Jackson crazy!

Sssh! It's a secret

Robby goes mad at Jackson for driving his car through a red light and getting a huge fine, but it turns out that it was actually Robby who was driving – doh-brain daddy!

What's your cringe?

....

....

....

Reach for the Stars

Robby is racing against time to get Hannah to her latest concert. Play with friends to see who can get them there first!

Rules

Take it in turns to roll the dice to move along the board. Follow any instructions you land on.

START

2

4

Sing the chorus from your fave Hannah Montana song. You've got another turn!

There's hardly any traffic! Go forward 3 spaces.

10

5

16

17

Make up a new dance routine for Hannah. Go forward 1 space.

Jackson is holding you up! Back to the start!

The limo's taken a wrong turn. Go back 3 spaces.

19

7

Act out a favourite scene from Hannah Montana. Go forward 2 spaces.

Hannah can't find her glove! Miss a turn.

8

13

FINISH

12

Robby has spilt a drink on Hannah's dress! Miss a turn.

Meet Oliver

Oliver Oscar Oken is Miley and Lilly's other best friend. He's Smokin' Oken!

FIVE FACTS ABOUT OLIVER

1. He's outgoing, flirty and fun!

2. He likes rapping, surfing and skating.

3. He's also called 'Locker Man' for his abliity to open school lockers.

4. He goes out with Lilly ...

5. ... but he used to have a massive crush on Hannah Montana!

smokin' shaven' Oken!

Oliver as Mike Standley III!

Here's Rico

Money-mad Rico runs Rico's Surf Shack. He's super-intelligent, but kinda annoying, too!

FIVE FUNNY THINGS ABOUT RICO

1. His totally evil laugh. Mwah-haha-haha!

2. His flirting— he even learns to line dance like a cowboy, just to impress a girl!

3. The way he gets really jealous when anyone else earns money!

4. His supersonic brain – he once finished a biology exam in less than one second!

5. His fights with Jackson. They're hilarious!

MWAH-HAHA-HAHA-HA!

service with a cheesy smile ...

Oliver & Rico's Best Bits

Oliver and Rico make us laugh a lot, right? Check out some of their funniest moments!

What a dummy!

When Rico ruined the dummy that Jackson was going to use for his ventriloquist show, Jackson came up with the perfect substitute – Rico! He totally looked the part as well!

Who's the boss?

Oliver drives Rico mad all the time, by insisting that he loves his job. So Rico once made him do all of the worst chores and even got him to dress up as a penguin to advertise the Surf Shack!

Too cool for school!

Oliver got loads of female attention after he was on, 'America's Top Talent'. He let it go to his head, but soon realised that Lilly meant more to him than his fans. It was really amusing when he strutted around the school corridors in his sunglasses like a superstar, though!

Meat Oliver

Oliver used to date a girl called Joanie. She was a strict vegetarian, so Oliver pretended he was, too. Then Rico put on loads of barbecues at the Surf Shack to wind Oliver up. It worked and Oliver ended up stuffing himself full of meat!

Dance with Daddy!

There were big laughs all round when Robby taught Rico to line-dance – they got the whole of Rico's Surf Shop to join in with them. Yee-haw!

SAVE OUR

Sticking together

Oliver, Jackson and Rico opened a package addressed to Robby, when he was away in Hawaii with Hannah. It was an inflatable house that blew up and filled the room as soon as they opened it, so they all got pinned against the window!

What's Your Celebrity Style?

If you were a celebrity, would you rock it like Hannah or be funky like Lola? Tick the fashion statements below that best describe your fave celebrity style.

1 I love coloured tights ☐

2 Short dresses with leggings are really cute ☐

3 I always wear loads of jewellery ☐

4 I like having one signature accessory ☐

5 Hair accessories are my thing ☐

6 Big, hooped earrings are really cool. ☐

7 I like to layer different fabrics and patterns ☐

8 Animal print is totally my style ☐

9 A wig can totally transform my look ☐

12 I love bold colours like red and purple ☐

10 I nearly always have a bit of pink in my outfit ☐

11 Plastic bangles and rings are really cool ☐

13 I adore vintage clothes ☐

14 Chunky boots and funky shoes rock my world ☐

Fashion Scene Queen!

Mostly Yellows
Your celeb style would be classic rock chick-chic with lashings of funky colours. You're not afraid to experiment, just like Hannah!

Mostly Blues
Standing out in a crowd is totally important to your style. What's the point of looking like everyone else, right? You're a Lola-style fashionista!

My Secret Album

"Hey, y'all, it's me, Miley! Take a sneaky peek at my photo album, but remember, don't tell anyone who I really am!"

I. cupid

Sweet niblets! This was such a super-cringe moment for me! I was playing a show in Vegas and I bumped into Traci and Jake. They told me they were getting married and I flipped out. I dressed up as cupid, pretending to be the Justice of Peace so I could break it off!

Gotcha!

This is when the camera crew turned up and I realised they'd been filming for a TV show called, 'Gotcha!'. They were totally pretending the whole time and it was all a set up! SO embarrassing, people! Especially as I then tried to prove to Jake that I didn't really care about him.

Honestly, Officer!

Uh-oh! Remember when I was arrested by a policeman for showing my Hannah Montana licence? I then had to prove that I really was Hannah Montana! His daughter was totally not convinced that I was Hannah until I started singing to her — phew, that got me out of a tight spot!

Goofball alert!

Ha ha! Jackson never learns does he? In this pic, he's fresh from trying to convince Alison he wasn't sick. She left after he sneezed on her — totally gross — and he ran outside after her, just as a massive storm broke. That is one soaking wet son-of-a-hill-billy!

So, not a good look!

Dang it, that car of Mamaw's is older than my daddy . . . and that is OLD! When she came to visit in her old banger, 'Loretta', Jackson and I got a face full of dirt when we tried to get Mamaw's bags out of the boot. That's when we decided it was time for her to get a new ride — turns out she didn't feel the same way about it, though!

Wigging out

Not my finest moment! We were at the mall and I wanted to let a shop assistant know that I'm Hannah Montana to see if I could get some freebies, so I decided to 'borrow' a little Hannah fan's wig. Kinda mean, I know, but her mom soon put me in my place. Yee doggies!

Blown away

There seems to be a running theme here of me embarrassing myself! Daddy had to clean me up using the leaf blower, after I fell into a giant make-up compact display at the mall . . . don't ask!

Talk to the hand

There's nothin' like a bit of freaky family interaction to kick start the day, is there, y'all? Check out my bro and dad talking to each other through their silly hand-face characters. This was Jackson's lame attempt to convince dad to let him go to a party. I usually just stick to my puppy-dog face – it works a treat!

What a doll!

OK, so I may love being Hannah Montana, but it's kinda weird when my best friend starts using a bubble-head doll version of Hannah to talk to me! That's Lilly for ya though, she's a kooky kinda gal – I guess that's why we're bffs. She gets my weirdness and I . . . put up with hers!

Eep!

I can't even look at this one! Ever since I was little, I've always had a ridiculously bad fear of the dentist. My usual dentist talks in kitty talk. Ya know – "Let me see your puuuuuuurrly whites." But this guy just wasn't pulling it off, and that needle!

Mini Hannah!

This was when I met a really cute guy called Connor who was shorter than me and I was trying to imagine what it would be like if I was a shorter version of me . . . strange I know, but it made me realise that things like that don't matter and Connor was my type, whether he was short, tall, fat, thin or whatever, y'all!

It's a Charade!

Grab your friends and have a giggle acting out Hannah Montana songs and episode titles! Here are some to get you started.

Episodes

1. Don't Go Breaking My Tooth
2. Knock Knock Knockin' on Jackson's Head
3. You Give Lunch a Bad Name
4. Miley Hurt the Feelings of the Radio Star
5. Can't Get Home to You Girl

Songs

1. Let's Do This
2. Supergirl
3. He Could Be the One
4. Mixed Up
5. I Wanna Know You

How to play

1. Write all of the song and episode titles onto scraps of paper. Fold them up and put them in a bowl.

2. Take turns to pick a piece of paper out of the bowl and without speaking, help your friends try to guess what the title is. Make it trickier by timing yourselves – three minutes each!

The person who guesses the most titles correctly, wins!

Imagine If ...

Have you ever wondered how different things would be if Lola was famous and Hannah wasn't? We've had some fun imagining a few other unlikely scenarios too!

Lilly was really, really quiet and shy!

Jackson was super-brainy and went to the best university in the USA!

Hannah Montana was a famous rapper, instead of a famous pop singer!

Rico won an employer of the year award!

Oliver was going out with Miley instead of Lilly!

Imagine a few more funny scenarios and write them down here . . .

1. ....

2. ....

3. ....

4. ....

How Well Do You Know Hannah Montana?

So, ya think you're a Hannah Montana expert? Test your knowledge with our totally cool quiz!

1

Who is this person?
a) Jack ☐
b) Jake ☐
c) Connor ☐

2

And who does he nearly marry for a joke as part of the TV series, 'Gotcha'?
a) Traci ☐
b) Lilly ☐
c) Hannah ☐

3

Where was Miley born?
a) California ☐
b) England ☐
c) Tennessee ☐

4

Robby loves to eat ...
a) Pie ☐
b) Lasagne ☐
c) Porridge ☐

5

What is Oliver's nickname for Lilly?
a) Lilly-pad ☐
b) Lilly-pop ☐
c) Lolly-pop ☐

6

Which of these films did Hannah star in?
a) Full Moontana ☐
b) Hannah Potter ☐
c) Indiana Joanie ☐

7 Oliver sometimes has a secret alter ego. What's his name?
a) Mike Standing III ☐
b) Mark Standley III ☐
c) Mike Standley III ☐

8 Which of these instruments can Hannah NOT play?
a) Saxophone ☐
b) Piano ☐
c) Guitar ☐

9 Who is known for their very distinctive laugh?
a) Jackson ☐
b) Rico ☐
c) Robby ☐

10 Who drove the Stewarts up the wall with their over-the-top cleaning antics?
a) Rico ☐
b) Oliver ☐
c) Lilly ☐

Play the quiz at your next sleepover to find out which of your friends is the biggest Hannah Montana fan!

HOW DID YOU DO?

Check the answers on page 68, then count up your points and check out your score below.

0 – 4 Never mind – at least you've got the perfect excuse to re-watch those Hannah Montana DVDs!

5 – 8 Good going. You're almost an expert. Re-read your annual and aim for top marks!

9 – 10 Awesome! You're top of the class! Are you sure your name isn't Miley?

Super Sudoku

HM

OO

Can you put each character's initials in the right place on the grid to complete the puzzle?

LT

The Rules
Each character can only appear once on each row, column and box! Get code cracking, y'all!

RS

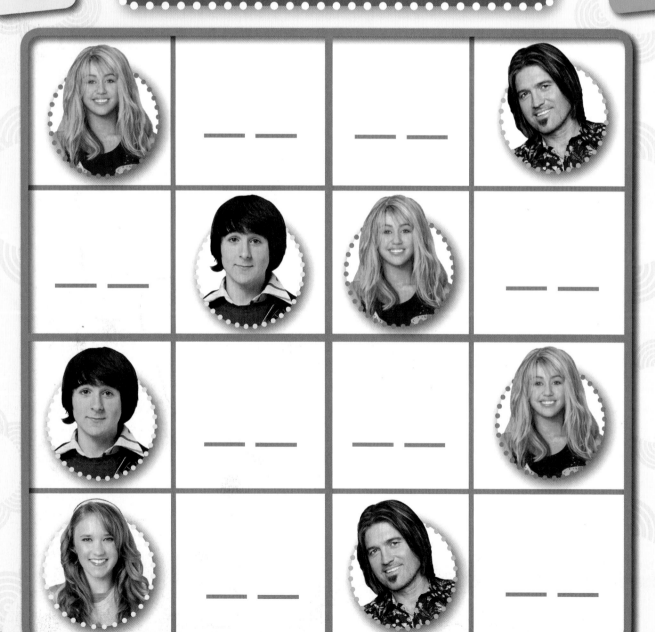

Answers on page 68.

Answers

11 Style Spot

1. Hannah 2. Lola 3. Jackson
4. Lilly 5. Robby

16 Miley's Music

17 Five Things

1. Hannah's belt 2. Lilly's hair
3. Jackson's collar 4. Lilly's badge
5. Hannah's bracelet

26 Picture Puzzles

Face Up!
1. Robby 2. Oliver 3. Lola
4. Hannah 5. Jackson

Shadow Show
Shadow C

27 Help Lola

32 The Missing Link

1. butter 2. pink 3. broken, 4. cold
5. friend 6. sleep 7. sweet 8. subtle
9. one. Hot doesn't appear in any of
the quotes!

35 Super Scramble!

1. He Could Be the One 2. I Wanna
Know You 3. Every Part of Me
4. If We Were a Movie

40 Say What?

1. Hannah in 'You Gotta Lose That Job'
2. Robby in 'The Wheel Near My Bed
(Keeps On Turning)'
3. Oliver in 'Judge Me Tender'
4. Lilly in 'I Honestly Love You (No,
Not You)'
5. Jackson in 'For (Give) a Little Bit'

42 Odd One Out

4

43 Word Whirl

1. For (give)a Little BIT **2.** Don't Go Breaking My TOOTH **3.** Miley HURT the Feelings of the Radio Star' **4.** Once, Twice, Three TIMES Afraidy, **5.** Ready, SET, Don't Drive

64 How well do you know Hannah Montana?

1. b **2.** a **3.** c **4.** a **5.** b **6.** c **7.** c **8.** a **9.** b **10.** c

66 Super Sudoku